SOUL ON STANDBY

SOUL ON STANDBY

Antony Di Nardo

Exile Editions

Publishers of singular
Fiction, Poetry, Translation, Drama, and Nonfiction

2010

Library and Archives Canada Cataloguing in Publication

Di Nardo, Antony
    Soul on standby / Antony Di Nardo.

Poems.

ISBN 978-1-55096-142-3

    I. Title.

PS8607.I535S68 2010   C811'.6   C2010-900780-8

Cover Photo by Vladimir Piskunov
Design and Composition by Digital ReproSet
Typeset in Bembo and Copperplate fonts at the Moons of Jupiter Studios
Printed in Canada by Imprimerie Gauvin

The publisher would like to acknowledge the financial assistance of
the Canada Council for the Arts and the Ontario Arts Council, which is
an agency of the Government of Ontario.

 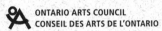

Conseil des Arts du Canada   Canada Council for the Arts   ONTARIO ARTS COUNCIL CONSEIL DES ARTS DE L'ONTARIO

Published in Canada in 2010 by Exile Editions Ltd.
144483 Southgate Road 14 ~ Gen Del
Holstein, Ontario, N0G 2A0
info@exileeditions.com
www.ExileEditions.com

Canadian Sales Distribution:
McArthur & Company
c/o Harper Collins
1995 Markham Road
Toronto, ON M1B 5M8
toll free: 1 800 387 0117

U.S. Sales Distribution:
Independent Publishers Group
814 North Franklin Street
Chicago, IL 60610
www.ipgbook.com
toll free: 1 800 888 4741

for Ann, again

CONTENTS

III. COUPLES

IV. Soul on Standby

THIS JUST HAPPENED

Monday, mid-July

Today the mind will play its tricks and have nothing to do with the weather.

A black wing borne by the wind, its beautiful spree in the air, settles on the neighbour's roof, turns out to be a plastic bag.

Things this real will never be the same again.

Like that blue pickup truck I've never seen this way before.

Island Island

The honey of limestone soft as light in a courtyard.

Lizards tagged in cut-out patterns stamped on walls.

A choir of cicadas on the airwaves 24/7 singing the same deliberate ringtones coming out of a crowd of trees.

Leaves soaked in sunlight and half-asleep.

There's been new fruit overnight, a succession of ripenings, pomegranate and lightning.

Fields of toasted wheat, acres and acres of king-size Shredded Wheat.

The stunted olive getting older, getting better, outliving us all with its own brand of medicine.

I'm on the coast trying to tie it all together with a pencil and a notebook.

Nothing can escape the page.

So much work for just a few words. For just another image.

This just happened

It starts again the moment I wake up and leave a good night's sleep mangled with the bedsheets. Every song I hear hits the right note, the water right out of the tap talks to the drain then drains perfectly away and disappears.

The geranium leaves, and the fern leaves and the veined cyclamen leaves collide and they're all the same colour.

A stone that's more in a state of pebble than rock delays being named, begs for a bed with the others. I'm here to speak on its behalf.

On the streets below after all these years they're still trying to make sense of Hamlet's philosophy even though they call it by another name. I heard Gertrude mentioned the other day and it wasn't pretty.

I have a walking stick that hasn't moved for years, a photograph taken of me that's not the same anymore, a poem on the tip of my tongue about to leap seven stories down.

There is no word for troll *in Slovenia*

Every true poet is a monster.
              —Tomaz Salamun

The Slovenian word for poet is *pesnik.*

A poet can go for days without water, but you can't make him think about anything else.

When he dies, you can expect his closet to be as empty as the soul he sets free.

A poet lives in the matter you find outside the village of his birth and between the temples of the state.

The Slovenian poet who teeters on the bridge he built with his own hands falls from a height one day and recovers the bottom of the pit he spanned.

Pesnik.

That's what they named the bridge because there is no word for *troll* in Slovenia.

Submission

There's always more than we bargained for.

When was the last time you paid a fair price for anything? Either way, someone's bound to get the short end.

First thing again this morning the coloratura canary across the way singing better than anything Verdi ever put to music or Battle up on stage.

What a voice! And that bird doesn't have a clue.

The day I heard my grandmother say I wrote so well, my penmanship went all to hell.

What to make of that? When in the flurry of rejections came the acceptance letter, nothing since has been the same.

White space

White affects us with the absoluteness of a great silence ... It's not a dead silence but one full of possibilities.
—WASSILY KANDINSKY

Because I'm made to think I know myself it's the same old, same old that steals the show every morning. Blue skies. Bright birds. The smell of coffee applauding.

More words to come to read and write.

To know thyself. What grand illusion from the brain's bazaar!

If I drop it altogether, kick it off the rooftop, ban the thought of it from the city of the self, drown it in the silence of a glass of beer, then there's nothing left to steal the show.

A touch of the disconsolate perhaps, the same defeated hairline, time's test of time, but not much else.

Already, as I lie here stretched out in the valley of my deceptions, I'm beginning to prefer the sky gone white, the clear-cut folds emptying the mountainside.

The beauty of a page left blank.

There are no truer souls than those who impersonate

Marilyn said to Michael, "Does anything ever really change? I mean, really change?"

"I don't know," said Michael. "I really don't know."

And then they loved each other sitting together in a chair and lying in bed, and walking arm in arm down the tracks, and dancing cheek to cheek. Most importantly, they loved each other cheek to cheek like in that song that says *heaven, I'm in heaven.*

It was a difficult day, but a beautiful one. There was some applause in the sky and the moon later that night was its own quiet miracle of light that made them think of another song they knew they could dance to.

Nonna dying

She is so well loved by the sky she thinks it feeds her bits of light to go on forever.

She grows lighter every day.

Her smile radiates mid-afternoon, her parchment skin translucent as a paper lantern, a halo with the silver hair.

She is like a wisp of smoke, weightless where she lies.

Beatific, says one who's been this close to death before.

Her breathing like a sparrow's.

She has always been this way, says a man of the cloth, as he draws the curtain shut.

And the sun keeps coming up.

Pandemic

Go long, one shouts
and it's 30 years later.
—Dean Young

To beat the swine flu you should wash your hands for 15-20 seconds as often as you can throughout the day, but especially after any human contact.

15-20 seconds is as long as it takes to sing Happy Birthday twice.

Whenever I sing Happy Birthday I sing it to myself. I mean, instead of singing "to you" I sing "to me."

Also, you should avoid touching yourself, especially the eyes, nose and mouth or any other orifice you might have exposed at the time.

But I digress.

What I mean to say is I'll be marking another birthday next week, another milestone I'm told, and I'll be sure to wash my hands several times that day as I think about how three decades ago friends and I were playing a pick-up game of touch in the park across from the house and I was running to catch a beautiful pass thrown in my direction, just yards from the goal line, when a bird dropped dead at my feet. It fell right out of the sky, just like that.

I think the team I was on lost the game that day, but that doesn't matter.

I could never get that little bird out of my mind. It was a sparrow – the kind you find all over the world.

At the foot of a sentry

These aren't birds but uniformed clouds.

And these aren't clouds but thoughts of taking battles back to war.

The soldier stands on guard outside a pathetic little sentry box and watches his part of the world come across the intersection or he slumps into a half-sitting position, leans against a storefront off the main street and sucks on a smoke.

He counts the garbage cats, sidewalk dogs, the cars on all fours. He adds up the number of times the giraffe with the flashing amber light in its head winks at him. The birds make it rain. It's a mash-up of a small menagerie but it's all he's got.

A soldier's world is out of his control. He knows when to take a break, the end of his shift, the ins and outs of his flight path home. Anything else won't make sense to anyone but him. The way he thinks about birds, for example.

Boredom is the number one enemy of the state. The battle is fierce. Too much of the same old same old at the foot of a sentry.

The last war he fought was out of complete boredom.

Why should the next one be any different?

Carpooling in Kabul

They can and cannot fly their kites.

You dig a well and the village comes out for a cup of tea and your shovel.

In the distance, the mountains dressed in flannels, the skin of goats and men, but still as cold as rocket fuel.

On the streets, a circus of old Trabants, even older Dodge Darts turn the corners and jump the traffic lights.

In the backseat, a cook, the maid, the bodyguard and the remains of your family in a plastic bag.

You leave them on the front step of the Ministry of Public Welfare and ring the doorbell.

I read a poem

by Stephen Dunn and one by Ilya Kaminsky that put me right in the middle
of an Italian town I once knew by Como or perhaps it was in the hills up from
Garda. No matter. There I was in the piazza with a glass of wine counting the
steeples – I was counting the steeples but they could have been towers – the
town, now I think of it, might have been outside Siena, a town of many towers
– and the pigeons of the piazza were strutting in the evening heat, swaying to
the rhythms the fountain played, its own half-mist half-obliterating the soldiers
cocking their rifles on the other side and allowing me to raise a glass to my
brothers dying in a film by Polanski while the rest of the world trudged for
hours in a circle with the familiar and the understood.

Springtime in Poland

He marched into Poland with a tourist visa.

In '82 even the linden trees trembled. A sky of soot and the only time for
sunlight was lost in the underground.

The cab driver who took cigarettes for a fare across the city and back. The
guide who whispered snatches of a history.

Half the seats at the Opera House, a Russian *Traviata* that night, were empty,
the other half with tickets in the state prison. The wardrobes reeked of
resistance and winter's end.

Vodka for breakfast. Empty bottles for the dinner's centrepiece. And with
watered-down borscht, the salami cut thinner and thinner.

In Krakow, he saw a stork on a chimney pot. The same on a postcard.

In Warsaw, the chambermaid who wanted nothing, only to touch.

But he gave her chocolates all the same, cigarettes, a western man for a night.

Beirut sunset

after Charles Simic

The vendor and his pushcart heaped with lemons who pushes them straight
into traffic and calls out your name. Who calls out for someone entirely
different.

The Romanian girls who sit, stuffed in a dingy microbus, bare-legged and
nubile, the vinyl gleam of heels and thighs. Who fan themselves on their way
to a late-night gig.

The car horns in the shape of an empty mouth that call out for God. And
God who answers them.

A remembrance of sprinklers past on the only lawn for blocks

He hears the trilling demi-chirp dip dip and swinging sudden sound of a
sprinkler's spurt that's out of sight but easy within earshot, its insistent spin
spin and spit is an insight into porch light summers and bygone Sundays
when all neighbours in the western world made it rain for their lawns, that
green bit parcel of less than an acre kept fit

for a picnic or a handy spread of dandelions left for the kids and the weed
pro killers, but for him, fisher of the lakes and of all tomorrows to come, the
lawns were then on loan for night crawlers he picked like nits and ticks out
of the hairs of a patch of grass, the fish a-jumping in his head.

And when it stops, the sudden sprinkling stops, the crumbs of a *madeleine*
materialize at his mouth and motorbikes mow down the memory, the car
horns blaring and rebar rattling, he returns to the heat and dust and fierce
blue sky of slab and concrete towers, the real and present absence of rain.

Stage directions for a dawn in West Beirut

Everything was sleeping as if the universe were a mistake.
—FERNANDO PESSOA, *The Book of Disquiet*

At sunrise before we ever get to see the sun rise, the mosque master takes the stairs to the top of his minaret – all of this in the fervor of his head – and pushes play on the Sony system installed with four loudspeakers, one for every corner of the world.

The track loops the customary lick – Allah be praised and raised above all – as in all the other narratives that we tell, sell or yell till we lose sight of the author.

But the spell is broken. The sublime silence that engulfed the city at night groans at the first sounds and stumbles into exile.

Now car horns, the drone of engines, the fuss of road and rubber, a few meek voices hurried.

The house lights blink, curtains drawn, the world has heard enough to bring it back to life.

And exeunt all.

In a book of foreign poems

I was in a bookstore in a foreign place where I found a book of foreign
poems with the Turkish on one side and the English full of plums and pears
and ripe figs on the trees

and a woman's arm reaching for another filling the basket someone had left
on a low stone wall to where the sea had sent an army once and the soldiers
came to stay with the women of the island who gladly gave them tongues
and other words to speak and all the fruit that they could eat.

Why would they ever want to leave this foreign place? An island fat with figs
and plums and ripened pears bursting in the flesh of their descendants who
turned the fruit back into poems, with the English on one side.

MOTHER MAY I

Mother may I

First one to touch Mother wins the game.
—from www.gameskidsplay.net

Mother may I take three giant steps?

Mother may I parachute and close the circle before you go?

Mother may I take a breath?

Mother may I move the room to the left?

Mother may I face the other way?

Mother may I stand on my head and see what you've done to the sky?

Mother may I reach for the door?

Mother, that hole in the wall. Why is little Tony hiding?

Antonio Luigi

Coppertone. Brylcreem. Pepsi Cola. Craven "A."
Wrigley's Gum. Chevrolet Impala. White House Motel. *Motel des Prairies*.
Velveeta. Aspirin. *Pain Durivage*.

The words came out loud from the backseat of the family car as they drove
out of the city and into farmland while his mother repeated the words like
she was learning to read.

But she wasn't.
She knew how to read.
He'd seen her with a box of cornflakes, Lipton soup.

All she was doing, she said, on Sundays driving into the country, was giving
the billboards back their names just as fast as he was taking them away.

Some game.

Like reading a word was thieving its soul.

Like naming a child was a power you couldn't forgive.

Some words I piece together to help me forget

A window overlooks and overcomes all feelings of wanting to be elsewhere.

I draw the curtains.

I draw the sun, the sky, and a few not-too-cumbersome clouds.

She smiles at me. I draw the blind.

When I leave the room, I leave Act One.
If I turn the page, I'm at the window again but I have no clue where I've been.
I just wanted to be elsewhere.

A rock comes through the window and nothing breaks.
Two birds build their nests in my head.
A tree quickly grows in my mother's mirror behind me.
The birds fly to the mirror.

Petite rue sans aventure

The bill collector came on Saturdays from Brown's Department Store not long after the newspaper boy and bread man had already taken some dollars out of the jar. One of them always with a toothpick in his mouth.

The first milk on the table was topped with cream causing a fight to break out in the kitchen. The radio voice screaming too loudly "love" and "you" by Dean Martin or Doris Day or Tino Rossi.

A sign at the end of the street said *Arret* with an accent on one of the vowels and a tree hung limpid over the corner.

Two big Impalas grazed by the curb across from each other, simple Dominique with the wax and buffing cloth before the sun got too hot.

The phone always off the hook in the telephone booth never rang. A broken bat that rested against the inside glass.

Two doors down, a neighbour who climbed to the roof to look for his son.

There was a house being built on the next block and a cement truck backing up on the street crushed a young boy's bike and his skull.

By day's end Dad came home from the bar with very little left of his overtime cash, a grudge and a case of beer.

That's when things really got started.

The Age of Reason

I wore my first green pants on *rue St. Denis* with a perfectly blue parrot on my shoulder, a scimitar in my belt, and in my hands a basket brimming with silkworms crawling on a matted bed of mulberry leaves like dewdrops in the sunlight.

I wore green pants on Atwater, red shoes with tie-dyed laces, and the goatherds on the sidewalks wrapped their heads in black and white *keffiyehs*.

I wore green pants at the corner of Mountain and Sherbrooke to pick up the ladies who were driving by in pink Cadillacs the summer of '68 when my hair was in a braid and my books were thin, just a few words on each page.

I wore green pants marching up to the gates of McGill speaking monosyllabic French and singing questions and equations we never answered or got to solve.

I wore green pants to dinner and no one noticed but my Marxist beard couldn't keep up with the soup.

And on Clark Street I wore green pants up the steps to my apartment and down the steps to storefronts configured by both the past and ethnic present with flags and crusty breads.

And green pants up the aisle and green pants on the beach and green pants to the office and green pants on my deathbed.

I wore the same green pants to heaven because I was told they were a gift from God, or that's what it said on the card. *On the occasion of your Confirmation, this is a gift from God.*

Merci, Mama. Merci, Papa. And I kissed them both on the cheek.

Dora in your life

Nobody can imagine how beautiful baby doll pajamas can be in moonlight unless you've also seen your favorite aunt wearing them to bed.

The night she took us in after our parents split.
If she held your face like she did mine, you'd know where I'm going with this.

When she asked would you rather sleep on the couch or in my bed, you could see how good you looked in the bedroom mirror.

Visions of Susanna Q.

Susanna Q. wore pink between her legs and the pages of the magazines on the floor of the shed behind her place were of naked women with earrings this big and beautiful heels on their feet.

She led me up sixteen steps to hold hands, turn the pages.

She had hurry-up lips and puppy dog eyes that I took to mean those forbidden places I would return to by moonlight by night by asking her for more of this.

One day borne by sunlight my mother came running up all sixteen steps in a wide-brim sun hat and nothing else was ever said about Susanna Q. after that.

Unhappy endings

The boy's father ran around with other women and the boy said to his father, stop that, it makes my mother look out the window of my bedroom when she talks to me and all her stories have unhappy endings.

The father said, okay, I will, but he continued to run around with other women and the boy's mother sat at the window trying to decide whether the rain that fell on the glass was anything like the tears she held back. Oh, those tears at the window!

But that was only a pathetic fallacy and she continued to tell the boy stories, each with an unhappy ending, until the boy became older and again he went to his father who was also getting older and told him to stop.

Okay, his father said again, and this time he meant it because he knew he was getting too old, like a leaky roof, to run around with other women, who were more like freshly painted steps that went right up to the front porch, and the boy finally understood where his father had been going all those years.

One day it was raining because it's always raining and the boy's mother took all the tears that she held back and put them in a glass jar which she threw at the bedroom window. Then the rain came in like little silver teardrops and the father said, you should sweep up the rain before you make the boy's dinner.

But he's gone, she said. Can't you see that he's busy running around with other women and he won't be back for dinner.

Okay, said the father, then tell me another story.

We also had pet birds in cages

As a child I was promised a new millennium of electric cars and communism,
instant food you pop like pills, and miracles of medicine.

I remember the day. Good Friday, 1959.

Hoisted from uncle to uncle they finally set my little sister down.
Even then her eyeglasses made her look smarter than all of us.

Our father who fell from heaven had bought that day half a dozen baby chicks
that he set in a cardboard box on the kitchen floor behind the door.

Lemon-yellow baby chicks for Easter cheeping through Good Friday.

By the next day they were all dead.

Mother said it was the flu.
Father cursed the farmer and turned his pockets out.
My little sister said it was all God's fault and in the future there would be no
God to hurt living things like that.

Especially us, my sister said. Especially us.

Gone Fishing

I never saw my father again after he died.

Mother came by a few times, once knocking on the bedroom window and in another dream she was out riding a bike like Butch Cassidy in that movie about Bolivia and raindrops and she had never ridden one before in her lifetime.

But my father stayed away. The "Gone Fishing" sign was a permanent thing for him. Alive, he'd cast for pickerel from the shore and always pulled in a disappointing pike too bony for the table.

Some things never change and stay that way for the better. Like his tackle box buried in the grime of the garage. I don't imagine I'd find a spinner or a spoon in there to lure him back from the dead. But you never know. He always said the pike was a better fighting fish.

What happens in cowboy movies

In Canada a farmer crops the fields, sows cows, corns the chickens and grows apples.
The land follows the eye to the very end of looking up to heaven.
The barn is by the gas station.
There's cabbage and potatoes.
The train goes on for years and then it stops coming.

That first summer of playing pennies on the tracks and feeding milk to snakes, the
farmer saw me doing a hangman's jig in one of his apple trees and he came running
after me.
I saw the farmer coming for me after I jumped and the rope in the apple tree
caught around my neck.
He saw me dangle inches from the ground.
I saw the space between life and death and what happens in cowboy movies only
inches from the ground.

As he ran towards me, the farmer's face got closer and his face was like another
version of my mother's, but he wasn't running like my mother.
My mother in her heels could never run like that.
Her face was running towards me and her mouth was saying things like "oh my
God."

But all I heard was the garble in my voice choking on words I had never made
before only inches from the ground.

When my mother cut me down with the farmer's knife she asked me if I'd like an
apple.
I said, no, Mother.
Can't you see I'm sleeping.

On the day no one came to visit

I wrote "there." Then "in a room" and then "a couch." Then I wrote "there in a room with a couch." And I waited for the animate.

I wrote "animate." But I was thinking "mother." There I was in a room. And I was thinking a couch is a permanence. In its place as it ever was. Not animate, but waiting for the animate.

Most importantly, a permanence. As there ever was a mother. Waiting for the animate.

There in a room with a couch.

Sestet, records, and that bastard Eric

I don't know how to begin to tell you this but it must be told.

Not for your sake, but mine.

That bastard Eric, *Eh-reek* as they called him, my cousin on the second floor who a week or so after we lovingly locked away my mother's ashes and the house was empty, slid through the bedroom window and into this story with a buddy. The two of them lifted the fireproof safe out of her closet and made away with her coin collection, her adoption papers and the first sestet of rhyming couplets I ever wrote, pencilled on a Mother's Day card.

There was no other record of our beginnings or a copy of that poem anywhere.

When I gave it to her, my mother thought it marked the start of a brilliant career. Six lines of metered rhymes. Of what words could do when tamed inside a card.

But that bastard Eric, high on crack, took it with him, all those words and silver coins, for just another night of obliterating bliss – obliterating any record of how this story really begins.

RPM

Into the gulag of the rec room our old man walks in wrecked and reeking rye.

It's an unrelenting 3 a.m., there's another record rolling to the beat of soul on the turntable, and he's got his own record to beat as he pumps his feet across the floor, smoke sparks and bared teeth missing, makes a meat cleaver with his fist and targets spinning the record player bull's eye of the 33.

Motown it was. It might have been Marvin Gaye hacked to bits, beat to a pulp.

Now we recollect the hi-fi shrapnel, black confetti record shit that hit the fan, the bits of R&B that night we picked out of our deep pile R&R.

You'd think the way we talk about it there'd been a revolution. Who thought then we'd ever live to tell.

A straight-up guy

He drank like a fish but had to quit.

An ulcerated stomach three-quarters gone doesn't leave much room for beer and boilermakers. A liver perforated by rye and gin doesn't leave much choice.

On a weekend he turned the downstairs bar – fixture of a '60s rec room – into aquaria. Glass tanks flanked by floating mirrors made everything all so clear.

He had to quit so he drank in the fish, taking in small gulps of matching coloured motions in seas of tap water, the fish weaving before his jaundiced eyes.

He likened the fish to mixed drinks he'd missed. Grasshoppers for the green ones flirting with shots of two-toned sambucas in a flaming B-52. The yellow ones he regarded as sun-filled daquiris and margaritas, caesars for the blood-red flecked ones, and for the bottle blues, names like Bols and de Kuyper.

Some say they stirred in him drinks he'd never had before having been a straight-up guy all his life. Beer and whiskey neat, a ghost of gin just that – a shot of crystal heat he could see right through.

But in the tropical world of his basement aquarium coloured veils and cocktail fins flashed before his eyes. He lied about missed opportunities, a wasted life. He had wanted so much more of the party drinks, the sweet savour of rainbows, less of the liquid storms.

It's all nature

I was raised on a balcony overlooking the city.

One, two, three, my father would say, and we're off to the country.

I'd ask him about the names of flowers, the yellow ones and the purple ones, and he'd answer in French, *les fleurs.* They were all the same to him.

One, two, three and sometimes *un, deux, trois* and he'd take us out to the sandy beach without ever leaving our balcony on *rue St. Denis.*

And those birds and those trees, what are they called? *La nature,* he'd say. It's all nature. My father, philosophical again, as we sat on the balcony overlooking the city and counted cars parked on the streets, those driving past. One, two, three.

And now that I'm here on this island in the Mediterranean, an improbable distance from where my father sat with us on the balcony, I name the exotic flowers, I know the birds that fly above because I've looked them up, and the trees are easy – palms and olives and the great cypresses of history – and they're the same as they've always been and the same as those my father talked about. There's really nothing more to add. It's all nature.

After the cemetery we all went to her party

After the cemetery we all went to her party and I took Death with me as my date. Everyone remarked how young she looked.

We wore black mostly, save for some flowers clearly in the act of dying.

"Red or white?" I offered.
"What do you think?" and she shot me one of those looks.

She sipped her wine as if sipping was an act of God, molecular, as she savoured each drop, drop by distinct drop.

I introduced her to my late uncle, Mort, but they already had a passing acquaintance. He straightened his tie before she even said a word.

Mother was known to frame her photos, so we framed the doorways with old snaps we found in a shoebox. As life of the party, a shame she was dead.

Death slipped her arm in mine and led me to a door.

"That's you in a sailor suit, isn't it?" She paused for a moment, her flaming hair lighting up the hallway. I told her the truth.

"So death by drowning it is then."

COUPLES

Couples

always move in pairs. If you see part of one, you'll see the other soon
enough. It's the way they follow each other.

Some are delicate and wistful – they breach the air like a pair of wings. Some
are Tarzan and Jane, grooming for nits and ticks.

Those two by the pool have been mating for years – it shows in the way
their bodies sag in the same places.

Favourable days and they rise together, spoons in bed, consider the matching
of sunrise and dawn as interchangeable as their lives.

They're the original bicycle built for two, a pair of aces, a damn good
two-for-one deal at the shops. They're the very essence of the Ark before the
flood, two peas in a pod.

They share the same destinations, dream in tandem.

They live on synchronized time, breakfast across from each other, go
barefoot, two left feet on the deck.

You'll easily pick them out in a crowd as you invent a life for them, their
conversations curled and contained in opened and closed quotations.

Summertime

We love you, says the collective noun of the garden.

We love you, too, from the birds who live on their own all day, then re-arrange their schedules when it's roosting time.

The cicadas may be shy, hidden among the leaves, but they are tireless in saying how much they love us, over and over and over again.

And don't forget how much we also love you, say the clouds on their way to somewhere else. Doubtless the sky loves you too, its overwhelming immensity meant to hang on to the sun and the stars when you see them.

Not a jealous word today. Only love is in the air. It's mid-July and so much of summer has gathered in one place it makes you want to snap your fingers and sing an old torch, admit to the world that the living's easy.

A piece of coloured glass

The sea is made up of more than the word for sea.

The hotel desk clerk stands at the counter and makes the sign of the waves
and it includes everything in the lobby. Everything.

The sky comes in at the double doors and there is light for a day in the
mirrors. I pick up the wind and the desk clerk says, yes, that too.

And what about the fishing village with the eaten-out boats? And the shade
of palm trees and the wall of bougainvillea that cheers the world?

That too, he says. And the church people and the tavern where the drinks
make you forget why the sea's this close.

In his pocket on a chain there's a piece of coloured glass and all the means to
open doors.

You'll need this, says the desk clerk.

And when I take it in my hands I wash upon the shore, something from the
sea, the steady cargo of the sun for ballast.

Billet-doux

These last three years I've wrapped up in a kerchief like a ring or a keepsake folded into the heart of the cotton and doubled two or three more times then tucked into the bottom of the top drawer of the dresser next to my other valuables such as a few ancient coins, our passports for when it's time for us to leave, a watch once mine that won't tell time, a silver tarnished bracelet you've never worn, and all the other years before these accumulated in a bundle of letters with those indelible postmarks that I can't read.

It's funny how three years can amount to a lifetime in a book or can change the course of history, whatever that means.

But three years in a kerchief, sweet with the scent still of your duty-free samples, well, that seems just about right to me.

Irrepressible love

The robin is in love with the worm and after days wandering the streets of Dublin a man falls in love with a beer.

Love is irrepressible like the wind that gathers up the leaves of autumn and gives them to someone else or like a very nice watch on your wrist that has nothing to do with time.

After old man Thibodeau fell through the ice, death was a warmth he had done without for too long and you could tell he loved the satin of the pillow for his head. But for the town, winter was a heartless bitch that year and it was forever before she left.

L, like the love song says, *is for the way you look at me…* and I like your karaoke version with the locking eyes.

Instead of a card that Christmas he gave his wife a dollar bill with a note that said, go get your own.

You wink and I send back, right quick, the *O-V-E*.

The plural of a pair

The foot, my foot, is exercise for an active mind.

All day it asks if it belongs to me or to the mortal world.

I came to see you in a pair of shoes but I would rather walk barefoot, it says.

A man makes trouble in combat boots. A woman has painted toes.

A man's foot rests upon the couch because he must eventually take it down from there.

A woman's foot is sometimes meant for sleep.

I heard your footsteps upon the stairs and they made the sound of coming closer.

Your shoes fill closets and every time I look they smile at me. If a cat could smile they'd purr as well.

Don't you think I know the difference between your foot and mine? I do. Yours is not meant to reach across the room, fill a ditch, kick pebbles at the moon.

Am I sexist when I say this? Of course, you exist like I exist. And I insist, the plural of a pair of feet comes before the both of us together.

Lovely and appropriate

I know a snakeskin when I see one, this one as long as six or seven lines of print.

A snake must have left it behind on the woodpile like I leave my shirt on the bed. What would his wife say? I know mine would make me hang it up in the closet, say something like all things in their place.

Yes, all things in their place. I'm not averse to order.

But that snakeskin looks fine to me just where it is, atop the woodpile mix of birch and maple.

The way the paper bark of the birch is lifting here and there, carelessly, like a shirt I might have tossed on the bed myself, it doesn't seem to mind the snakeskin either, which I think is lovely and appropriate for the last week of holidays, before bells begin to ring again, before I shed my T's and shorts for a shirt and tie.

S.S. Friendship

That friends come and go might be true and said about all of us whether we're at the receiving end or not. There's something of the fickle moon in that, the undecided storm clouds.

That friends happen suddenly, even accidentally, two people pushed into the same boat by forces neither or only one of them understands, has also crossed my mind.

That friends ferry their friendship back and forth across the bay only so long until one of them stays behind or the boat capsizes, can happen to anyone.

Songs and poems are full of that.

John, who could quote a good line or two about true love and eternity, made the crossing all on his own one day. I stayed behind.

Or was I the one who never showed up at the dock? It's hard to say. I certainly don't remember ever waving good-bye to him.

I suppose one of us just forgot to tell the other where he was going that day.

And still somehow I wonder if he even bothered to wait for me before he pulled away.

Parts and labour

The bigger part of his heart was the dump truck that had been up and down the road all morning loading and unloading dirt from the neighbour's backyard.

Her heart left long ago in the Camaro when it still needed new brakes.

They had met at a flashing red light. She was riding a flat. He had the jack in his trunk.

Their first kiss was a high beam in a parking lot by the GM dealership.

At their wedding the limos wore white. When he signed the register he looked up at her, the highway still in their eyes, and asked about a warranty. She was smiling, laughing, kicking at his tires. Whitewalls.

Two years, and they were slamming doors. The overhead light burnt out. Fill-ups got more and more expensive. A new transmission would cost them.

There were no trade-ins. The lot was empty.

He was up on the hoist for a rusting of the bladder.

Her shocks were shot pulling all-nighters and the back and forth.

Back at home he had his own set of wheels on a chair that took him from the bedroom to the front door window.

His time was up.

Her timing was all wrong.

The windshield wipers stuck on intermittent the day she left.

At the window, the dump truck in his eyes had been up and down the road all morning.

His heartbreak poems

In the book of the heart there is no mention made of plumbing.
—RUSSELL EDSON

That's one more poem too personal for me. He's fiddling with tongues and tears and the work of other wet places until some other body part goes missing.

Now he's looking for her hand to grip or twist and snap right off so he can place it on the bedside table, a match for his own hand, he says, when he needs someone to hold, to find a fit and call it his.

I heard a Western twang in that.

He goes on. His poems go on.

A lover's quarrel, a break-up at the Barrie Inn ends up in bloodstained walls, mosquitoes whacked to death with a section of *The Globe*.

He longs for her lips, cut-outs of her mouth around the vanity mirror so he can work his face like hers, rehearse her lips on his, a bitten lip with a bit of blood. It becomes too much.

In a poem all thumbs and backseat sex, he's got her fingerprints on the dashboard to remember the night.

He jumps a traffic light and hurdles screeching into her arms while she's not there. A long embrace that brings her back intact belongs in a scene by Tarantino where the body goes missing.

All kinds of weather in a poem.

Any kind of weather is okay for a poem or for love or money, but storms brood like crows in his, coo like doves, stink of skunk for the sake of a simile that subverts all loveliness.

Or is it all loneliness?

Comes a point when the words don't matter much.

It's raining, his heart is soaked, her flesh dissolved, what more need be said?

The hotel room

It's made for two. Most are made for two.

This one rides you to the top and reaches eye level with a break in the mountains, the moon last night.

You can imagine how well the sky surrounds you at the summit – you feel yourself surrounded by something so why not let it be the sky.

She thrusts a knee into the sheets. Still asleep she slowly moves morning into a shape I begin to understand, into why we're here, why I'm here.

Last night I knew this room better than anyone else. I commanded the light switch, the TV remote, the opening and closing of the curtains. Every nuance of this room was my kingdom waiting for its finest hour.

I knew what was to come.

Now the morning light casts a different scene, the bedsheets confused, the anarchy of our clothes scattered outside the rule of law a rented room imposes.

The past, barely six or seven hours old, rewrites itself as an ancient history I must explain.

That door – once an entrance, now the only way out.

The enigma of the missing person in a future perfect tense

Ann disappeared this morning in a puff of smoke and waves of goodbyes, left for an ashram in India.

It was a common feat – by taxi and flight – leaving behind all of December that was yet to come.

She left it up to me – four weeks of the future perfect tense to fit the space her singular soul once occupied, the places her meditations silenced.

Four weeks and four walls, to keep the incense burning, open windows, find the right words when I talk to myself.

Such is the enigma of the missing person, of putting the past in the future, that by the time she's back I will have filled in all the blanks that she left empty.

The Brits

There are more than you think.

You'll find them hidden here and there with suitcases stacked in closets next to those daily papers of theirs that state and restate the world.

Those with a grin have been drinking. They're full of good cheer toasting a thousand years of life with the Magna Carta.

Their wit is beyond reproach – they've made the best of it with only one language to their name.

It's the rest of the world that needs a second language. The Brits are born with it.

They've had ships criss-cross the globe and British Air. At discount fares they're everywhere, even in the bedrooms of your friends.

Across the table, sipping tea or a pint with their chips, that's them. Say, hullo. They'll give you all the time in the world.

It's theirs to give.

Sometimes real life is not a pretty sight

They kissed into each other's sadness on the platform in Cornwall, a
nothing town on the river like he was a nothing guy, his ball cap turned
peak backwards and the chain around his neck made of metal bones a link
to all his buddies in the gang singing the same old tune and she, well, she
was going east and she could have been pretty except he was smeared all
over her lips and her eyes were running like muddy water in a ditch.

When the train left the station the first thing it did was bound across the
bridge like she had jumped on board and I leapt to the conclusion that I
felt nothing for them – nothing of that sadness or why it should have ended
this way between them.

No empathy at all.

I was just another smiley on a fat balloon about to float a world away.

Ferdinand's

At times a snowfall is only that, then there is the one that changes your mind and the sky is falling because there is no other reasonable explanation like the metaphor in your pocket that is eating you up and wants to get out.

But there are others.

For example, when doubt is sown into the couple holding hands at the barroom window and they see a circus of cut-out paper flakes and paper faces charging past Ferdinand's on a Friday night, everyone else oblivious, was that the wind or the vodka at last?

Ferdinand's is the kind of place you find on Earth where combinations of smoke and mirrors work to reassign what stands for what.

Like that trick of hers when she melts into the crowd and disappears.

Asymmetry

My words, you said, are asymmetrical, you can't find any meaning in them.

Meaning, I said, isn't that when the gods kneel down to us and pray we make them mortal? I can't do that to them.

Or should I find meaning in the astrology department at U of Fools, when Mercury rising and the Moon in your house determine how the rest of your day unfolds?

Well, how about this, then, something deep-seated and real?

I've got a zillion zeros in my head and you're the only one.

SOUL ON STANDBY

India

India survives in our minds on the illusions the rest of the world has of her.

We all would love to bathe in a holy river, the fabric of our lives clinging to our thighs.

We'd love to throw handfuls of tinted powders at each other, laugh about it, ruin a good set of clothes.

We could easily endure a fast, go without for days, then lick our fingers clean, make every morsel count.

We seek the anonymity of the crowded markets, hang our lives on a thread from the rail of a train that leaves the station late.

We like the air of cardamom and cinnamon we breathe from each other's bodies when we're lashed to the midday sun.

We all expect to cross the fields on foot from one village to the next, the luxury of an only book in our pockets that we've read and reread.

The other day I told a friend my best poem is always the last one I write.

India, with its temples, gods and nightingales, is like that too, the last place we visit and always the first one on the list.

Variations on "Frère Jacques"

Should've counted them last time I went up the steps the pilgrims took to see the brother's heart encased in glass.

Should've held my father's hand a little tighter that day then maybe he wouldn't have run off with the lady standing at the counter in the souvenir shop.

Should've listened to the dead man's prayers, whose encounters were legend, his prayer pose perfect, whose words stirred a people to build a dome at the top of the mount.

Should've walked the Stations of the Cross a second time, counteracted my impulse to climb up to the summit, stopped to take another look at the fifth and the seventh.

Should've left home sooner, gone astray faster on a boat, on a westbound train, let the Count of the Montrose Theatre run his hands up my thigh a little higher.

Should've leaned in closer when the Latin hung limpid and lovely above the pews, replaced so suddenly by the discount language of the vernacular, whose mother tongue we already had.

Should've marked my own place in the firmament above the city by Beaver Lake, held my head high for the Seven Sisters of St. Joseph recounting that time when we sang the chorus in a round and it only worked when the trees joined in.

Should've, could've on account of my age asked forgiveness for my sins but morning bells were ringing as I climbed steeple-top and I saw beauty in the world when I looked down below, a beauty I couldn't put into any of the words I had at the time.

Of guns and gods

No guns, I promised.

I know. I know how you feel about them on the streets, in the movies.

Last night we saw one without any guns at all, and that's exactly what you liked about it.

But we all know a thing or two about guns and what a good gripping story they make. Even a well-paced romantic comedy can benefit from a loaded pistol left on the mantelpiece.

No gods, I promised.

I know how you feel about those too.

No *deus ex machina* to hinder the progress of a plot.

But you must know about Montreal and its oratory, Mont Royal topped with a cupola and a couple of saints.

I want you to see for yourself what I saw first-hand for the first time in a childhood caught in a web of prayers when we prayed on Sundays only. It left quite the impression, that visit to the oratory.

I was crippled into faith at the sight of all the wooden crutches, prostheses and hernia belts that hung from the altar in the chapel of miracles, Bakelite body parts that decked the halls and dimensioned the walls. I was on my knees in the face of creation's lapse, fear of a God who was hell on earth for me, my own severed limbs imagined and served up to the saints as I pissed my pants.

I didn't know it then, but I've made sure that trembling moment would never repeat itself, the memory poised on its own two feet, loaded and ready to shoot to kill if it must.

And, yes, I know, I'm sorry.

Louise Bourgeois

It is not so much where my motivation comes from, but rather how it manages to survive.

Such a simple poet, I dream one day of dedicating a poem to one of my contemporaries because I happen to have sat across from him or her at a dinner party and we had a stimulating exchange of ideas or I couldn't resist the press of her breasts against her blouse and said so.

I'm reading about them in their books, their poems like miniature helicopters high among the rag of clouds that tear and clarify a vision or they're like flies that just won't land or leave.

I think Karen Solie could be hot, her lips just so with the utterance of an image I could never imagine all on my own.

And I don't know what I'd say to Charles Simic or Ken Babstock, but I'd like to think the words would come and I could borrow something brilliant from some other late night composition or conversation I've had with myself.

Like some time ago at the Guggenheim an ancient artist spiraled her work from the bottom up and I could follow the thread of its unravelling into a poem. I liked best her later years exhibited on the upper floors – she was 90 or more at the time – and she filled cupboards and closets with scraps and remnants of ideas she had run out of things to do with and reified. There were bloated mannequins, bolts of brocaded fabrics, patterned paper samples that spoke riddles, spools of threads like spiders keep if they live to be a 100 – her family had been in the textile business – old machine parts, brass cogs and wheels exposed, connected cables, salvaged memorabilia sculpted out of wood and words, and sentences cut out and pasted on walls or stitched together or flashed in neon colours on a screen. It was cluttered with a lifetime of work and I was overwhelmed. I had the feeling I could sit with her in her 5th Avenue apartment, have a sherry perhaps, and discuss her next project, look over some sketches, ask about *Maman* at the National Gallery. You must go and see *Maman*.

I'm making most of this up from memory, of course, as I write for the sake of a poem and a poet – that day at the Guggenheim curled at my feet – but there's no doubt in my mind so did she for the sake of her work.

For the birds

The canaries on the neighbour's balcony can keep a song going for hours.
Whenever I look up, there's another pigeon that writes a byline across the sky.
In the window box, a dove sitting on her eggs, placid as a rocking chair.
Over by a distant wall, a black bird perched on a TV aerial, listens for the latest.
An only airplane strays into the sky above me.
A car horn suggests a tension on the streets below.

The birds take no notice of the man on stilts.
If there's an accordion playing somewhere, I can't hear it.
The man on stilts is barely moving.
He's only standing there, balancing on his two wooden towers.

Perhaps if he heard the accordion …

Sundays on the rooftop there are more birds than people that come and go in
this city.
The canaries' songs won't stop, doves are cooing soft cones of beauty.
Another bird that I can't see, along with the rest of its kind, is reciting a poetry
I think I've heard before.

There's the chatter of birds everywhere.
I'm sure they're all leaning closer to listen.
They have the city to themselves.
They own the skies.

Best of all, when they call it quits they don't even know it.
They just come and go as they please.

Lucky them.

That's normal

We've been paddling on the river without a paddle for many years now.

You ask for a paddle that I don't have and I say I can't give you what I don't have.
We are happiest this way.
You equally reciprocate my request for a paddle that you don't have.

We are happiest this way because we are all on the river without a paddle.
Because the river is our paddle we cannot give the river away.
Not until we get to where we're going which is and always has been our only destination.
Where the river takes us is where we all end up, without a paddle.
Then the river is ours to give and those about to reach their destination are happy to receive it.
That's how it works.

It's better this way, say the people at the front.
Those at the back, the youngest and the latest, also agree.
Because we all equally agree it's better this way.
We all know it's better to be on the river.

The riversides run in the opposite direction, but sometimes also in the same direction depending on how one thinks about it. That's normal.

But you can't change direction when you're on the river without a paddle.
It's better to look ahead and have happy thoughts.
The river knows where it's taking us and there's no need to know anything else.

Go with the flow, is on everyone's mind and on some people's T-shirt.
Some wear white, some wear black, many are in reds and blues, some striped
in yesterday's rainbow.
It's a beautiful river – long for some, too short for others.
But in time we all get to where we're going. We all do. That's normal.

Overtime at the koan factory

When a door opens in the known universe, another one slams shut in the unknown.

The sound of one hand clapping is what you heard when you were born.

Last night I walked into the shadow of a street lamp and disappeared around the corner.

Can you match this? Here for the grace of God, or as a reasonable facsimile.

My maritime mood is like my mind made up of red skies in the morning and all the words I ever read going out to sea.

All the wisdom of a koan is in the way it bites its tail.

"Ah, description," wrote Charles Wright, "of all the arts the least appreciated."

In the meantime. I'll just leave you with this.

Official adjectives

Eyes have only four or five official adjectives: brown, blue, hazel, green.
—John Berger

There aren't many others standardized for other parts of the body or, for that matter, the journey from A to Z.

Hair? Perhaps, but nothing official, nothing that takes into account losing a full head of it or going grey.

Eyes, your eyes and mine, maintain that official status throughout. They may be limpid or glassy, piercing or misty, the sleepy shape of almonds, but the green ones stay green.

I can't think of anything official in the scope of stars and suns. They're either on or off. Nothing official to describe the birds. Species and measurements, yes, but they pale as adjectives. Trees are accustomed to the full treatment of language, as are cups and couches, the door to your garden. They survive in their modifiers.

Sure, a metaphor can be a beautiful thing to reflect your eyes and some poets have been driven wild by their lover's.

But officially? If I check your papers where does it say eyes deep as the pools of Lethe where I go to forget?

Newsreel

Clocks have been falling from the sky throughout the day in three-quarter time – 1-2-3, 1-2-3 – like World War II bomblets we'd see in those old black-and-white newsreels.

You'd hold my hand, and I would hold my breath.

How old could we have been as we watched the beginning of the end of the world?

I'm certain now we are both of some indeterminate age, time with the unlikely face of a clock in a free fall from the sky and chasing us back into our useless shelters.

Portrait of a soul on standby

As I sat down to drink a cup of oolong tea on a couch by Vermeer

and considered the consequences related to losing a lifetime of unlimited
access to a God created in the image of a Plasticine clock

I was flattened

and left to distinguish the two-dimensional from the mirror

Lucian Freud looked into when he said, *what could be more surreal than a nose
between two eyes?*

Georges Braque was here

I love to see the high-wire spirit of a flock of birds rise and circle above the distant rooftops, like tickertape, confetti, a moment you should hold your breath for.

The way they rise and circle unexpectedly all in the same motion, swim in the air with the same swipe of wings, a quick stroke of the brush against the blue canvas of an impression.

But concrete and blue sky, that's the beauty of the city when nothing moves.

Dabs of grey and marginal slabs of yellowed whitewashed blocks dried in a cubist revival, a still life on a grand scale—

man with mobile and satellite dish, window with gutters and guitar, rooftop shadows descending stairs,

and at my window, a trace of mourning doves arrested in mid-flight, the stutter of an architectural composition.

As autumn begins to pink

As autumn begins to *prink* is what Wright wrote but I read *pink* and I
thought I could pinch a poem out of that line,

piggy-back it on the one he named, "Autumn Is Visionary, Summer's the
Same Old Stuff," but there's no half-moon in mine and no clouds like Turner
saw.

All I could write about was a thin memory of leaves turning in the literal
afterglow of a sunset.

That, and the thought of being nowhere close to the mountains of my
hometown where autumn's likely fallen off the map by now and pink is
altogether the wrong colour.

An ordinary evening elsewhere in New Haven, reprieve

The assignment was critical. I had to identify all the fruit ever named, grown, pitched, picked, eaten or left to rot in a Wallace Stevens poem.

I stopped at the mango.

Because the mango decides for itself how the air surrounds it.
Because its flesh is corn bread and bits of sun.
Because it dreams of loam and mountain flesh.
Because I thought so.

The mango arrived at mango-ness all on its own.

A mango picks you out from the others in a crowd in front of a supermarket shelf.

A mango resists what rhymes with itself, but loves to dance on tables, that careful beam of light undressing it, a distant castanet.

The right of return for a mango? Remove it from its self-appointed place in the known universe and see what happens.

I stopped at the mango.

And the mango stopped for me.

The looking fee

Two came from the garden, the other out of nowhere. They multiplied forth so many times that kings and queens were needed, and wooden wheels and wheels of fortune and ways to raise a wall. It is difficult to imagine, but it was never enough.

The wheels have changed but they are turning still, bringing footwear and furnishings to all beings who live beneath the kings and queens who spin the wheels and then sit still to write their stories. In this world there's always one who sits while others toil, cavort, go off and die forgotten.

There is a door to this garden. It's painted green and sometimes black, sometimes red and white and sometimes blue, and then all over again the colours change like colours changing on a flag depending who is king and who is queen. So many coats of paint, the door is hidden, perhaps it's lost, and only a flag prevents us all from entering.

But no one thinks of going back. Why bother? There are sufficient words outside the walls to keep us busy for a very long time. Those who've seen the garden in their dreams charge a small looking fee. Not too much, just a lifetime of believing.

How science sometimes imitates art

There are too many people with degrees, says the farmer. And too many scientists multiplying like the variety of fruits you find now in the supermarkets. Did you ever buy a mango or a lychee nut when you were a child? I sure didn't.

The audience applauds because they are a good audience.

I will show you how smart I am, says the farmer and the farmer performs a scientific demonstration even though he doesn't have a degree. He's at the podium, wearing a lab coat of which he is proud. Proud as a papaya, remarks his wife.

This, he says, is how science works. And he takes a baby volunteer from the front row and buries him in a pot of potassium-enriched soil.

This, he says, is for demonstration purposes only. A field of several fertilized acres is the best medium for planting babies and to make them grow. Furrows should be five to six feet apart and a baby seed likewise planted every five to six feet, what I'd say is the average height of an adult person. A five by five configuration, however, is the preferred pattern, for both ease of feeding and weeding. It is also important to know that as the babies grow they are to be touched as much as possible. This will encourage pollination in the adult stage. Water them generously. Weeds can be treated with a regimen consisting of a few swift kicks, Dr. Phil philosophies and daily prayers. Observe this slide.

And he was right. A twenty-five-acre field revealed a perfect checkerboard pattern of heads sprouting from the earth, a veritable work of art, which the farmer said could be harvested in 8-10 months.

Someone in the back row said, wow, look at that, it's the Madonna and Child by Rubens.

Liar, liar

I'm not much of an actor though I can tell a good lie and I've always wondered if there could be a part for me to play in something like *Cat on a Hot Tin Roof* or my all-time favourite, *Hamlet*.

In *Hamlet* I'd see myself in a minor role, a gravedigger perhaps or one of the poor players who struts his stuff upon the stage in front of the king and gets him to catch his breath, as Hamlet had hoped, and snap the trap of his own deceit.

I could also be that king for the king would need to be a convincing liar, at least in the first two acts as we, the actors, execute our lines and establish the plot of where this mother of all tragedies is going.

However, knowing my temperament I'd be most suited to the irony of a gravedigger who with a wink and a "What, me worry?" look says right to your face that there is no getting old in death so get on with it and jump in. I could be like the all-in-one wit and wise guy hit of the play.

But in *Cat on a Hot Tin Roof* I'd expect to play the lead. Yes, definitely the lead.

At the Piggery in North Hatley

where the Beatles performed. Four men dressed in tailored suits like the Beatles performed songs by the Beatles when those songs were on the airwaves for all time, four young men in suits for whom the young girls swooned in crowds that gathered at the foot of the whole wide world, calling out all manner of epithets of love and new and strange desires, these girls who had never had their empty spaces filled before by any young man's flood or any of the Beatles until they came on stage and sang a song never sung before yet everyone knew the words since they were humming them in their heads before the show even began.

The whales in that dream

and singing backup for the Stones, is all I can think of these days.

These days. That's a curious way to put it. Certainly closer than *those days* pushed further back into a greener time.

But these days trail right behind me or run up ahead and have me catching up to them.

Wherever they're going, I'm with them all the way.

Like the whales in that dream. I couldn't take my eyes off them, the way they swung their tails high into the air above the bay, the slick surface breaking into fountain, the sea sliding off their backs, the glisten of the rubber of their skins. I could go on, they were so beautiful.

Eye-popping, alright. A pod of giants. I opened my eyes that morning just to remember them like that.

And singing backup for the Stones? Well, let's say these days I've also got rock and roll on my mind, moving to the beat of Charlie Watts

and singing doo-wap deep in the shadows where I can be heard but barely seen, all eyes on Jagger and Richards, just like the whales in that dream.

Zippo

I'm so envious of poets who can use the word *Zippo* in a poem like they really mean it.

I've never owned one, so my experience is limited.

But to write *Zippo* and have the whole poem wrapped around your little finger, now that's something.

That's the kind of word that could very well resurrect the Age of the Literary Salon, instill a Tarantino clip in a runaway dream or bring us back to a bar scene in the '60s before non-smoking by-laws put us out on a patio.

I think sometimes of my predilection for fire.

I say *Zippo* and I'm Neolithic, banging rocks to make a tool of me, fascinated by my own opposable thumbs, running back to the hut brandishing a torch, my soul on fire.

My Ars Poetica

I love a good poem as much as the next guy.

Okay, so these sounds don't make an extraordinary music and the meter's not what you expect twisted in its own hermetic knot, but look at all these words and spaces — isn't this some poem?

Such beauty in a declarative sentence.

So surreal to have the ineffable plainly stated.

Like the bishop singing to the crickets at his graveside. Or the first woman James Tate puts on the moon and has her disappear in a poof of tangerine dust.

Back on earth we're experts at following the fall of a leaf, its broken lines crystallizing in a lyric we can't get out of our heads. But is that all we're here for?

There must be more to the west wind when it blows.

Poetry II

Poetry, unhurried, chewed slowly, drawn deeply in, is proven to lower cholesterol by 14%.

Taken daily, the benefit to the heart is incalculable.

Though no guarantee of longevity, poetry, whether read to oneself or out loud in the woods, in the gardens by a river or on the steps of city hall can restore damaged tissue and prolong, if only for a moment, a life lived well, sustain the pageant of accumulated years.

Notes & Acknowledgements

Louise Bourgeois' sculpture of a giant spider she titled *Maman* is located in the esplanade outside the National Art Gallery in Ottawa. You must go and see *Maman*.

In "As autumn begins to pink" the poem by Charles Wright to which I refer is from *Sestets* (Farrar, Straus and Giroux 2009).

In "My Ars Poetica" the poem by James Tate to which I allude is "Cherubic" in *The Ghost Soldiers* (Ecco 2008).

★

My thanks to Barry Callaghan at Exile who took several of the poems found in the "Mother May I" section for publication in the journal, *Exile: The Literary Quarterly*.

★

I am indebted once again to Rania Jaber for reading these poems so many times and in so many ways. And for her tireless enthusiasm and friendship.

And to Susan Briscoe, who knows so well how to temper one's prose.

This book is dedicated to Ann, as always, who one day said to me, "Somewhere in that equation there's you."

Antony Di Nardo was born in Montreal and has lived in northwestern Ontario, Toronto, Germany, and Beirut. His poetry appears widely in journals across Canada and internationally. Both writer and teacher, he was editor of a small town Ontario weekly newspaper, contributed fiction reviews to *Books in Canada*, and writes fiction and non-fiction content for educational texts. He is the author of the collection, *Alien, Correspondent*.